BEATING BU...

HOW TO BEAT CYBERBULLYING

JUDY MONROE PETERSON

rosen publishing's
rosen central

NEW YORK

Published in 2013 by The Rosen Publishing Group, Inc.
29 East 21st Street, New York, NY 10010

Copyright © 2013 by The Rosen Publishing Group, Inc.

First Edition

Library of Congress Cataloging-in-Publication Data

Peterson, Judy Monroe.
How to beat cyberbullying/Judy Monroe Peterson. — 1st ed.
      p. cm. — (Beating bullying)
Includes bibliographical references and index.
ISBN 978-1-4488-6810-0 (library binding) —
ISBN 978-1-4488-6817-9 (pbk.) —
ISBN 978-1-4488-6818-6 (6-pack)
1. Cyberbullying — Prevention. 2. Cyberbullying. I. Title.
HV6773.15.C92P48 2013
302.34'3 — dc23

                                                                2011043256

Manufactured in the United States of America

CPSIA Compliance Information: Batch #S12YA: For further information, contact Rosen Publishing, New York, New York, at 1-800-237-9932.

CONTENTS

Bullying is when someone or a group of people says or does hurtful things to gain power over another person. In person, bullies can hassle someone in many ways, including verbal abuse. They also might trip, push, hit, or kick their targets in school, on the playground, or in other places. Sometimes, they break or steal things that a victim owns.

Using computers, cell phones, and other electronic devices to bully is called cyberbullying. Many people use these tools to stay in touch with family and friends, find information, or listen to music. However, cyberbullies use these electronic devices to embarrass, harass, or threaten someone. They might attack over and over, day or night. Cyberbullies use words or pictures to scare or taunt their targets at home, school, or anywhere. Victims feel threatened because they cannot escape the attacks and may not know their attacker.

Examples of cyberbullying are spreading rumors and lies, name-calling, teasing or scaring someone, or telling secrets. Cyberbullying occurs in many ways, such as through the use of unwanted and rude e-mail, instant messaging, text messaging, and wall posts. Some teens write hurtful comments about others on blogs. Cyberbullies might take embarrassing videos of someone with their cell phones and send the videos to others or post them on YouTube.

According to the National Crime Prevention Association, cyberbullying affects about half of the teens in the United States. Cyberbullying is upsetting and painful for the victim. Sometimes, it Is one of the main causes for teen depression that might result in suicide, or taking one's life. Bullycide is the act of killing oneself purposely as a result of bullying.

In middle school, Jamey Rodemeyer of Buffalo, New York, was ridiculed and taunted because he liked being with girls. Some of his classmates tormented him for being gay. In May 2011, Jamey posted a video on YouTube about his bullying and spoke about help that is available for gay teens who are bullied. After starting high school that fall, Jamey seemed happier. He did not, however, tell his family that he continued to be bullied. The high school freshman wrote about his despair in a blog. On September 18, Jamey committed suicide in the backyard of the family home.

Because teens often carry cell phones and keep them turned on, they can be constant targets for cyberbullies who text mean comments.

When caught, cyberbullies may be pulled from sports teams or suspended or expelled from school. Sometimes, bullies make hateful online comments about someone's religion, race, gender, or physical differences. This type of cyberbullying is harassment. Because harassment is against the law, cyberbullies could face legal trouble.

Teens can learn smart ways to protect themselves when using electronic devices and how to stand up for themselves, friends, and others. Everyone should feel safe from cyberbullies and also learn how to stop cyberbullying.

CHAPTER 1

BULLYING AROUND THE CLOCK

Unlike traditional bullying, cyberbullying can occur at any time and affects victims in many ways. Cyber victims often feel angry, embarrassed, or scared. They may become depressed and experience hopelessness, helplessness, and sadness. Some teens feel isolated and believe they have few or no friends. Certain cyber victims find it difficult to talk about their true feelings.

HOW CYBER VICTIMS FEEL

Victims who are afraid or depressed can lose concentration and not do well on homework and tests. As a result, their grades drop. Others might have problems falling or staying asleep, have headaches or stomachaches, or get sick often. Sometimes, they gain or lose weight. Some cyber targets feel anxious and jumpy. They might shake and sweat and their heart might pound.

Many targets may feel stressed when receiving e-mails or e-messages, using chat rooms, or gaming online. Some may stop using their e-mail or avoid using computers or cell phones. Other victims will not talk about their Internet activity with anyone.

Some targets of cyberbullying drop out of school activities or sports teams or stop going to school. They may lose interest in hobbies and friends, have low energy, and have difficulty making decisions. Those who are depressed might abuse alcohol or other drugs or drive recklessly. Sometimes, victims need to change schools to escape their cyberbullies. In extreme cases, particular targets may feel the only way out of depression is to commit suicide.

THE TARGETS OF CYBERBULLIES

Young people being mean to one another by using the computer or phone may begin as early as the second grade. Fifteen is the average age of cyberbully victims. Girls are more likely to be targets than boys, and older girls receive more online threats than older boys.

Teens who are different in some way or have behaviors that others find annoying or amusing are likely to become victims of cyberbullying. Cyberbullying victims may have low self-esteem and feel insecure. Some may not have the social skills and the ability to communicate to stop cyberbullying or get help. Many victims are not assertive or do not know how to stand up for themselves. For example, some teens feel they will be tattling and get someone in trouble if they report cyberbullying.

The more time teens spend on the Internet, the more likely they are to experience cyberbullying. Online activities include getting and sending e-messages and photos, using Facebook, sharing artwork or music, building Web sites, or Internet gaming.

Sometimes, targets fight back by striking out at their cyberbullies. They fire off angry e-mails or post nasty online comments on blogs, Facebook, or Myspace. Then they become bullies themselves. Cyberbullying can increase quickly. Responding in anger only puts other bullies on the Internet or cell phones.

Social networking sites allow people to share ideas, activities, events, and interests. These sites also make it possible for a cyberbully to target a person without having to meet face-to-face.

ONLINE CYBERBULLYING

Any type of bullying or harassment that occurs on the Internet, cell phones, or personal digital assistants is cyberbullying. A common type of cyberbullying is sending mean or threatening e-mails, instant messages (IMs), or text messages to hurt someone. Some teens may also take private e-mails or messages and forward them to others or post them on Web sites or blogs to embarrass another person. They might share conversations with others without permission or create insulting Web sites or blogs. Numerous bullies use Facebook, Myspace, or Twitter to spread rumors, insults, and lies or to make fun of somebody. Cyberbullies may put embarrassing photos or videos of their targets in e-mails or on YouTube, Facebook, or Myspace.

Some teens have more than one account on social networks. They may use one that is for their family and relatives and another one to bully people. Others might create a fake online person to trick people into telling them personal information. For example, a shy boy might not know that an online person is really a bully and confide that he has a

A sender's tone when sending a text message may be difficult to detect. As a result, one person's joke sent by text messaging can be insulting to another person.

crush on a popular girl. The bully would then forward this information for others to read. Some bullies hack into a teen's profile and pretend to be that teen to cause problems. These cyberbullies might spread lies about someone to make that person look bad or get into trouble.

Bullying can cross the line into harassment, including cyber threats and cyberstalking. Threatening to harm someone is a cyber threat. Criminal laws against making cyber threats are in place. Cyberstalking is repeated harassment such as using the Internet to follow and observe someone in a threatening way, which causes the victim to feel very fearful.

People cyberbully for many reasons. It can be teasing that gets out of hand and turns into taunts and jeers. A grudge held by a victim might turn into revenge. Peer pressure might cause someone to step into the role of cyberbully. Some teen cyberbullies might mimic cruel behavior they see in a movie, TV show, or video on YouTube, or experienced themselves. Other teens use the Internet or cell phone to deliberately hurt someone by their words or actions.

CHAT ROOMS, BLOGS, AND BASH BOARDS

Cyber abuse can occur in chat rooms where people chat back and forth by sending and receiving messages. Most teens usually use screen names (also called usernames or nicknames, which are made-up names), which are posted on each other's computer

USING CELL PHONES TO BULLY

Most teens usually keep their cell phones turned on. This makes the cell phone an easy tool for bullies because they can continually target a person. The victim can't get away from the harassment. Bullies might send constant threatening text messages to a person at any hour. With cell phones, people might forward a private text message, photo, or video to someone else. Or they may capture someone changing in the locker room and instantly send the embarrassing video or photos to other cell phones or e-mail accounts or post them online. Sometimes, bullies alter photos or videos to humiliate the target. Once a photo is sent electronically, no one knows where it will be posted, how it might be changed, or what will be said about it. Moreover, things posted on the Internet can still be found there years later.

screen. Messages appear instantly. Everyone in a chat room can read all the messages and send replies, unless the users "go private" and have an IM chat. Sometimes, cyberbullies post mean messages about someone in a chat room for everyone to read.

Blogs are another way bullies can get to victims. People can read and write about a person or topic by adding comments to the blog. Some cyberbullies post hateful remarks about others on blogs.

Bash boards are online bulletin boards where people post their thoughts and opinions about other people. Many bash board

Cyberbullying can go viral, which means a large number of people are aware of the bullying via the Internet. Being disrespectful is one of the most common forms of cyberbullying.

postings make fun of people. Some bullies put up rude cartoons, drawings, or photos of their targets.

ONLINE GAMING

Many teens enjoy online or interactive gaming. Online gaming can attract cyberbullies who might taunt and tease beginners as they learn the game. They may continue to harass someone who has responded to their initial attacks or pretend to be someone else and make up lies about teens or other gamers.

EXCLUSION

A teen can be bullied without directly interacting with the bully. For example, a cyberbully might delete a teen from a friend's buddy list to make that teen feel left out. Or, a bully can lock someone out from everyone's messaging servers. The excluded person feels degraded and alone because of being isolated from the others.

A cyberbully might exclude a teen from Facebook, Myspace, Twitter, or other social networking sites. Bullies then build a community in which its members know what is going on in the victim's life. They might post hurtful e-messages, pictures, or videos about the teen victim.

CHAPTER 2

THE MANY FACES OF CYBERBULLIES

All cyberbullies have a reason for their behavior. Some may feel bad about themselves and think being a bully will help them feel better. Cyberbullies want to upset, hurt, or scare other people to feel superior and powerful. They want power over someone at any cost, or they seek a sense of control and attention by striking out at others. Using computers or cell phones allows them to reach their targets at any time. These electronic devices can also provide bullies a wider audience than only the target.

WHO ARE CYBERBULLIES?

Exactly who is a cyberbully is somewhat unknown because no single accepted definition of cyberbullying is in place in the United States. In addition, many people remain anonymous until caught. They can hide their identity by using temporary e-mail accounts and phony chat room names. The cyberbullies are then faceless, and victims can't see their real name, phone number, or address.

The majority of cyberbullies know their targets. They may crave having power over their targets, especially if they, too, are being bullied.

Cyberbullies are usually preteens and teens, although they can be people of any age. If savvy with technology, they can remain hidden while harming others. Most cyberbullies know their victim either in person or online. The target may be a classmate, a current or former friend, a relative, and so on. Some cyberbullies become familiar with their target from a chat room or online game. People might also cross the line with something they write or show on the Internet or a cell phone. Sometimes, what one person thinks is a joke could be insulting to someone else.

BYSTANDERS TO CYBERBULLYING

Bystanders are not bullies or victims, but they witness cyberbullying taking place. They may know it is wrong but not take any action to stop the bully or to help the victim. By their inaction, they give approval for the cyberbully to continue his or her improper behavior. For example, teens might pass around embarrassing e-mails, text messages, or IMs. Such actions openly encourage the bully who sent out the messages. Some people write nasty comments on a bash board that a bully has created. Other teens read rude e-mails and e-messages or look at embarrassing photos of someone but do not pass them on. However, by doing nothing, bystanders are part of the cyberbullying and are not being respectful and kind to the victims.

A number of factors or situations can increase the risk of a teen becoming a cyberbully. However, having one or more of these does not always mean that a teen will become a bully. Some factors that can have an effect include having poor self-control and poor parenting by caregivers, and feeling that it is OK to be cruel or violent. Abusing others is a way for some cyberbullies to cope with difficult situations at home, school, or work.

USING ELECTRONIC DEVICES

Knowing how cyberbullies work can help many teens deal with a bully. Cyberbullies do not physically hit or kick a target. With technology, they hurt people's feelings and make them feel unsafe and scared. When people think they cannot be seen or found out on the Internet, they may do things they would never do in person. Some teens mistakenly believe that bullying online is nothing serious. The ease of cyberbullying may appeal to them. People can instantly release put-downs, rumors, gossip, and embarrassing photos in e-mails, blogs, and chat rooms. For example, a girl might send a stream of nasty text messages to her former boyfriend

Teens who have disabilities are often targets of people who engage in bullying because they may be seen as being different from others.

after a painful break up. People can change electronic photos or videos to show something about an individual that is embarrassing or untrue. With a few clicks, one person can post hurtful words or pictures to a few or thousands of viewers.

Some cyberbullies know that using the Internet can make it difficult to trace and find them. Computers can easily allow people to be anonymous, enabling bullies to hurt their victims without seeing them in person. In addition, many teens are not supervised by adults when using the Internet or cell phones. This lack of attention can lead cyberbullies to feel that they can be hurtful to their victims and will not get caught by their parents or authorities.

By using the Internet and cell phones, bullies can get to teens at home, including evenings and weekends. They can attack repeatedly. Even if a bully stops, it may be difficult or impossible to remove all the mean online electronic messages or photos. Cyberbullies may not take down cruel photos or posts on Web sites or blogs when asked to do so.

FEMALE AND MALE CYBERBULLIES

Female and male teens tend to cyberbully in different ways. Girl cyberbullies prefer to share personal information about their targets. They are more likely to write mean and upsetting e-mails, IMs, and text messages. By spreading rumors and gossip, they can damage another teen's social life. Girls who bully usually harass victims on cell phones instead of on the Internet.

Boy cyberbullies more often make direct threats online to get revenge on someone else. They are more apt to tease and call their target names one-on-one. Boys typically use the computer to cyberbully. For example, they might hack into a victim's computer and steal passwords. They tend to use their cell phones to pass around hurtful photos, drawings, or other images of their target. Boys, more than girls, use exclusion to cyberbully.

HURTFUL TO VICTIMS

All forms of cyberbullying are harmful to victims. Teens feel they cannot hide or have no way to escape from cyberbullies, even at home. They can be attacked online day or night, and they might not know what is being said about them or who is behind the cyberbullying. Targets might fear for their safety because of continual online threats and harassment.

Repeated bullying can cause victims to feel tense, afraid, and anxious. Teen victims might have more health problems, such as headaches, stomachaches, and colds. They can have mood difficulties and be hostile, angry, or irritable. Some cry often and easily. The self-esteem of victims may decrease, leading to feelings of worthlessness.

Some targets do not report cyberbullying and keep their problem a secret. They think they can handle the taunts and teasing

Cyberbullying leaves no physical scars, but the hurt it causes can be very severe. Targets of cyberbullying often feel alone, which can lead to depression and anxiety.

themselves. Some feel weak and unpopular or are too embarrassed to speak up. Sometimes, they think they have done something wrong and worry they will be punished. Victims may fear revenge from their bullies. Another concern is that adults will not take their complaints seriously or will react in upsetting ways, such as taking away their cell phones or computers.

Such secrecy can cause teens to feel alone. The effects might be long lasting and can include depression, anxiety, drug abuse, and abuse of family members. Targets of cyberbullying may withdraw and drop out of school activities, clubs, or sports teams, or not want to go to school. They lose interest in hobbies and friends, have low energy, and have difficulty concentrating and making decisions. Victims of cyberbullying might react by arriving at school very late or very early and avoiding school or activities. Sometimes, teen victims run away from home. Others feel that the only way out of their depression is to commit suicide.

 MYTH   Cyberbullies are often popular, smart, and attractive.

FACT   Cyberbullies can be anyone, girls or boys, teens or adults. Everyone and anyone can be cyberbullied.

MYTH   Bystanders to cyberbullying are not affected in any way.

FACT   Many bystanders to cyberbullying do not feel good about themselves and can become troubled or sad. Bystanders, the bully, and the victim will not feel proud of their actions. All experience harm in some way when cyberbullying occurs.

MYTH   Most teens cyberbully to get revenge on someone.

FACT   Many teens think cyberbullying is funny or a way to play a joke on someone. Some teens cyberbully because they think their peers do it. Also, friends might encourage someone to cyberbully. Bullies may not realize the negative effects of their actions.

CHAPTER 3

STANDING UP TO CYBERBULLYING

Teens can protect themselves from cyberbullies. They can plan ahead so they will know what to do. When people feel upset or scared while on the Internet or cell phone, they can take action to stop the bullies, including asking for help. Teens should be open to getting help and can also help others who are being cyberbullied.

PREVENTING CYBERBULLYING

Being careful while using the Internet and cell phones is important for everyone. Cyberbullies can reach people only if they know how to find them. Teens should not give out personal information such as passwords to anyone online, not even a friend. Someone who can get or guess a password can then pose as that teen. Only parents or another trusted adult should know a teen's passwords. Many teens change their passwords regularly.

After an online bully made nasty comments about the photo that was on her Myspace page, this teen posted a new photo in response.

Other personal information that someone should not see online include a physical description, phone number, address, birth date, Social Security number, driver's license number, school name, or bank and credit numbers. Teens probably should not open e-mail, IMs, or text messages from someone they do not know. It could be spam, which might contain upsetting messages or viruses that can destroy computer information or shut down the computer. If teens decide to message or chat with someone they do not know, they should not tell their age, address, or any other personal information.

Myspace, Facebook, and many other online social networks allow teens to set up a profile to tell about themselves. Teens should not enter their age, phone number, home address, or school on their profile or other postings. They can choose an icon to use for profiles instead of posting personal photos. Online social networking, e-mail, and instant messaging sites allow teens to set limits on the people they can chat or message with by using privacy settings. Some online games also have privacy settings.

Teens need to be careful about the people they put on their friends and buddy lists. Friends can save, copy, rewrite, and repost whatever teens put on a social networking site, Web site, or blog. Teens should be responsible by asking if it is OK to post pictures of their friends.

CHOOSING STRONG USERNAMES AND PASSWORDS

Many e-mail, networking, and gaming sites ask people to choose a username and password. Having usernames and passwords that others cannot easily guess can protect against cyberbullies. Teens should not use their real names as their usernames because every-one on a site can see usernames.

A strong password is seven to sixteen characters in length and includes lower- and upper-case letters, numbers, punctuation marks, and other characters. Avoid passwords based on diction-ary terms, usernames, relative or pet names, telephone numbers, birthdays, and other information that may be readily known or easy to guess. To create a password, some teens think of an uncommon phrase or short sentence and take the first, second, or last letter of each word. They turn these letters into their password by adding special characters near the beginning, middle, or end of the letters. Words, letters, or characters should not be repeated in a row, such as in the passwords "deskdesk" or "11B2wtt." Some Web sites tell how strong a password is when creating one. Following these instructions can help keep people safe.

If teens think that someone else knows their password, they should change it right away. People should not write down and keep their passwords where others can easily find them.

RESPONDING TO CYBERBULLIES

People deal with cyberbullying in different ways. Sometimes, they can take care of the cyberbullying on their own by ignoring the bully or deleting the bully's messages without reading them. Cyberbullies may give up if they do not get a response. Another option is to log off from e-mail or instant or text messaging, or shut off the cell phone. Changing usernames, e-mail addresses, or passwords might keep a bully away. Limiting computer and cell phone time is another good step. Teens may want to get a new cell phone number.

A bully can be blocked on e-mail sites, IM lists, Web sites, and social networking sites. Photos, pictures, and other images can also be blocked on e-mail sites. Teens should receive e-mails only from people in their address book or from people they know. When using a buddy list for IM or social network sites, people can be blocked based on their username. They can also be removed from a buddy list.

Sometimes, the real names of anonymous bullies can be figured out. Bullies tend to use the same words in person as they do online in their e-mails or messages. Their messages might include things they have done in person. That information provides clues about the identity of the bullies. Most cyberbullies are or were very close to the victim.

GETTING HELP

Some cyberbullies will not back down, causing teens to feel scared or distressed. However, they are not alone and can get help. Telling someone is important. Teens can tell a parent or another trusted adult, such as a relative, teacher, coach, guidance counselor, or youth group leader. People should never be afraid to speak up or feel cyberbullying is their fault. Teens should be honest about their experiences and any steps they have taken to deal with the bullies.

The best source of help in dealing with cyberbullies is another person. People who are targeted should not feel they need to deal with the situation by themselves.

Victims should not respond to cyberbullies. Instead, they can save any abusive or nasty e-mails, e-messages, and photos. They can print or forward the messages to an adult's phone. They can take screenshots to capture comments cyberbullies make in a chat room, an online gaming site, or a message board. Targets should also keep track of the date and time of a bully's activities in a journal or log. Recording the names of everyone who sends bullying messages is important because cyberbullies sometimes use several names.

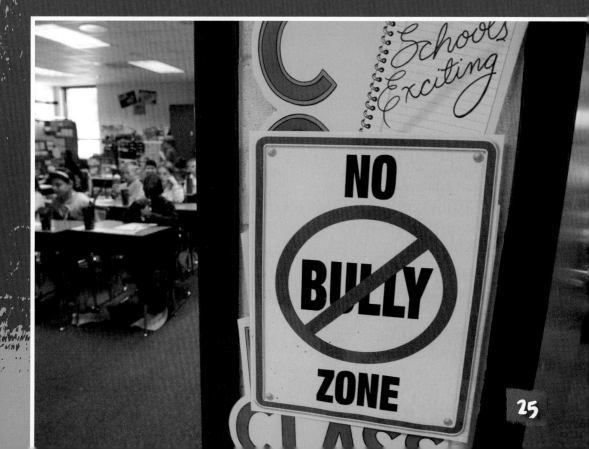

Many schools post warning signs prohibiting bullying at the school or on school property. The signs are symbols demonstrating that teachers will help targets of cyberbullying if needed.

AT SCHOOL

If cyberbullied at school, students should report it. There might be a bullying box for reporting such incidents available at school. Students can explain the problem even when they do not know or want to say who the bullies are. Some schools have a bullying court that deals with bullying. Teachers and other staff members are usually not involved. Many schools have an antibullying policy and rules that discuss how it will deal with acts of bullying. The policy is available for all students at school and may also be available to read online. Guidance counselors are a good resource. They are trained to deal with bullying online, in school, and on school grounds.

INFORMING INTERNET SERVICE PROVIDERS

Bullies might change their e-mail address or not use their real name. Computer bullies often can be tracked down. All computers on the Internet have an Internet protocol (IP) address. An IP address usually is a set of four groups of numbers, such as 555.14.54.936.

An IP address is in the headers of e-mails. The header also includes information about the message, such as the identity of the sender, who received the message, the date and time the message was sent, and the subject of the message. The full header of e-mails is usually hidden. Teens or adults can determine the full header to find out the route the e-mail took to reach someone, including the original IP address of the cyberbullies.

Armed with this information, people can report bullies to their Internet service provider (ISP). ISPs host Web sites. They have rules about what people can and cannot do on Web sites. Adults can call or e-mail the ISP and ask them to deal with online bullies. People who have broken the rules can get booted off a site.

TELLING CHAT HOSTS

Teens who stick with chat rooms monitored by a person are provided with some safety. Usually the chat host checks the activities on the site to keep messages safe. The host polices the site and kicks off cyberbullies. Teens, though, need to report bullies. The messages between people are private, and the host cannot read them. It is up to teens to keep track of what cyberbullies write and then pass the information to the host.

HANDLING ONLINE GAME BULLIES

If bullies strike during online gaming, victims can stop playing the game for a while. They should also tell the people who run the game site about the cyberbullying. Some sites will allow teens to create a game to play only with invited players.

ENDING CELL PHONE HARASSMENT

Bullying by phone can take the form of nasty or silent phone calls or mean text messages. Teens can tell the abuser to stop calling or sending messages. Sometimes, the cyberbully is anonymous. Teens should keep all threatening messages and let a trusted adult know about them. The adult can contact the phone network. People there can find the bully's network and block the phone used to send the messages. The cyberbully's account can also be suspended from the phone network. Young people who are harassed by phone should make sure they seek professional help with an adult's assistance.

10 GREAT QUESTIONS to ask a guidance counselor

 1 What is the first thing I should do if I receive threatening e-mails or text messages?

 2 When should I call the police if I receive threatening messages?

 3 Is it OK to send a mean e-mail to someone who cyberbullies me?

 4 Should I ignore someone who is cyberbullying me?

 5 Is it OK to use my cell phone if someone is texting mean messages to me?

 6 Can an anonymous cyberbully be traced?

 7 A friend sent me a rude e-mail about a classmate. What should I do?

 8 What should I do if I think a friend is being cyberbullied?

 9 How do I know if I am being a tattletale when telling someone about a cyberbully?

 10 How do I know if I'm being a cyberbully?

CHAPTER 4

CYBERBULLYING SOLUTIONS

In 2011, forty-seven states had antibullying laws. Some of these states have updated and improved their older antibullying laws to include cyberbullying. Although cyberbullying is a newer problem than bullying, it is getting increased attention from the government, schools, organizations, and the media.

CYBERBULLYING AND THE LAW

Congress has considered laws that would make cyberbullying a federal crime. One bill, known as the Megan Meier Cyberbullying Prevention Act, has been before Congress in 2009 and 2010, but it has not passed into law. The bill may be brought to Congress in the future.

Some U.S. states have laws against cyberbullying, such as California, New Jersey, Missouri, New York, Rhode Island, and Maryland. At least seven states have passed laws against cyber harrassment since 2007. California was one of the first states to pass legislation on cyberbullying. The law went into effect on January 1, 2009. Under the law, schools can discipline

Tyler Clementi apparently committed suicide shortly after he was secretly videotaped in his dorm room and the video was streamed online.

students for bullying others online. In addition, some cities have made online harassment a crime.

Since 2010, public schools in New Jersey must follow the Anti-Bullying Bill of Rights. Some people think it is the strongest such law in the United States. The law was created and passed, in part, because of Tyler Clementi, a student at Rutgers University's Piscataway, New Jersey, campus. Without asking permission, his roommate and another student used a Webcam to spy on Clementi and another man kissing in his dorm room and then streamed the video over the Internet. Clementi committed suicide soon afterward.

WHAT SCHOOLS ARE DOING ABOUT CYBERBULLYING

In some states, teachers are required to report bullying. However, schools usually have limited authority to handle cyberbullying if it occurs after school hours or off school grounds. If the cyberbullying is happening at school and is reported, school administrators

Through its Cyberbullying Resource Center, the Anti-Defamation League (ADL) and its Web site (www.adl.org) supply information about cyberbullying for teens, families, and communities.

probably will handle the situation. Peer counseling can be offered to the victim. If the cyberbullying escalates and becomes constant, the school may involve the parents so that they can work to stop the behavior. The bullies could be suspended or expelled from school. In serious situations, the police could become involved.

Some schools provide ongoing programs that help create a healthy social climate while students are in school. Kids at every grade level are taught how to be leaders and to be concerned about others. They also teach victims good ways of dealing with bullies.

Many schools are adopting bullying prevention programs that are provided by various organizations. One example is the Olweus Bullying Prevention Program by the Hazelden Foundation in Minnesota. Schools in many different countries have used this program for more than twenty years. The program focuses on preventing or reducing bullying at the school, classroom, and individual levels.

Another example is the Anti-Defamation League (ADL). This organization works throughout the world to raise awareness of bullying through technology. The ADL stresses that schools should have clear policies on cyberbullying that include training for all staff. In addition, the ADL promotes bullying prevention laws in all states.

Through the organization Students Against Violence Everywhere (SAVE), students learn cyberbullying information and prevention. Then they practice what they learn about nonviolence and conflict management skills through school and community service projects. For more than ten years, Web Wise Kids (WWK) has taught students and parents about the dangers of using the Internet and cell phones. WWK creates realistic and interactive computer games to reach teens and adults. To date, more than ten million middle and high school teens have been involved in WWK programs.

OTHER CYBERBULLYING RESOURCES

The Web site StopBullying.gov by the U.S. Department of Health and Human Services provides information from government agencies on how to prevent or stop bullying. It provides a list of resources for teens and their parents.

Sometimes, teens feel desperate about being cyberbullied and think they cannot talk to anyone. They may think about suicide because of their unbearable pain. Teens can call hotlines any time, day or night. All calls are confidential. The specially trained staff provides immediate support by listening to callers and discussing their

Cyberbullying has increased in recent years. Online information provided by the federal government at www.stopbullying.gov, and a growing number of organizations offer information on what cyberbullying is and how to stop it.

problems. If requested, staff can provide advice and tell teens where to go for more help. These hotlines are always open, and the call is free.

INDIVIDUAL RESPONSIBILITY

Even though the Internet may not feel like the real world, there are rules about how to behave online. If teens break these rules, they could lose their e-mail, IM, or Internet account. They could get into serious trouble with the law.

Seventeen-year-old John Otto spoke about his suffering through bullying. He was with a group who stood outside the New Jersey State House as lawmakers worked to toughen the state's antibullying laws.

Teens should make sure their e-messages are kind and respectful. One way to do this is to avoid gossiping, passing on or starting rumors, or harassing others online. When a person is feeling upset or angry over a message, it is a good idea for that person not to respond right away. Another idea is for teens to write a message and read it aloud to hear how it will sound to the reader. Or, they can count to ten and read their message again. Before pushing the send button, teens should try to picture the reader's reaction. They do not want the reader to feel angry, sad, or confused when seeing the message. In addition, teens should be careful before posting or sending messages or photos because those items could be used later by a bully to hurt them.

THE MEGAN MEIER CYBERBULLYING PREVENTION ACT

In 2006, thirteen-year-old Megan Meier of Dardenne Prairie, Missouri, had just started eighth grade and was on the school volleyball team. Megan met Josh Evans on Myspace and they quickly became online friends. In October, Josh started to send cruel e-mails to Megan. Soon mean bulletins about Megan were posted online. Deeply upset over the cyberbullying, the teen committed suicide three weeks before her fourteenth birthday. Megan's parents tried to message Josh, but his e-mail account had disappeared. Later, the police discovered that Josh was not real. The mother of one of Megan's former friends and another teen had made him up. Meier's story was widely reported on the Internet. On May 22, 2008, Linda T. Sanchez, U.S. representative from California, and Kenny Hulshof, U.S. representative from Missouri, cosponsored H.R. 6123, the Megan Meier Cyberbullying Prevention Act, to change the federal laws concerning cyberbullying. They introduced the bill hoping to make cyberbullying a federal offense that required cyberbullies to be fined and/or imprisoned for at most two years.

How each person acts on computers or cell phones is critical. People might want to say mean things to others online, especially if they get upset over a rude or embarrassing e-mail or e-message. Some teens may think it is fair to bully back. However, this reaction would only put another cyberbully on the Internet or cell phones. Teens can fight cyberbullying by joining the antiviolence programs at their school, community center, local clubs, or religious organizations. If their school or community does not have a program, they could ask a teacher or guidance counselor to organize classmates into an antibullying group or club. Although raising awareness about cyberbullying must start with the individual, antibullying clubs can provide concrete information about the dangers of cyberspace, the effects of bullying, and effective ways to combat cyberbullies.

anonymous Not identified by name; of unknown name.

assertive Having or showing a confident and forceful personality.

bash board An online bulletin board on which individuals can post anything they want. Generally, posts are hateful statements directed against another person.

block To deny access. A person blocked from joining a chat usually receives a message that says access has been denied.

blog A journal or diary published online instantly.

buddy list A collection of names or handles of friends or "buddies" within an instant-messaging or chat program.

bullying Hostile behavior or intentional harm done by one person or a group generally carried out repeatedly over time.

bystander A person who does not take part in an activity but watches or does not act to stop it.

chat An online conversation, typically carried out by people who use nicknames instead of their real names. A person can read messages from others in the chat room and type in and send in his or her own messages in reply.

chat room A virtual room where groups of people send and receive messages. All of the people in the room are listed by their screen names somewhere on the screen.

cyberbullying Intentionally harming somebody through electronic text or a technological device.

cyberstalking Repeatedly following a victim around chat rooms or repeatedly sending e-mails or text messages, or calling a victim so that the victim feels there is no escape.

cyber threat Message sent through the Internet or a cell phone that is intended to inflict harm or violence on someone else.

e-mail Electronic mail that allows Internet users to send and receive electronic text to and from other Internet users.

e-message An electronic or text message sent via the Internet or on a cell phone.

exclusion The act of not including someone in an online group, such as a buddy list.

harassment Words or actions intended to annoy, alarm, or abuse another individual.

hotline A telephone line that provides support for a particular type of problem.

instant messaging (IM) The act of instantly communicating between two or more people over the Internet.

Internet A worldwide network of computers communicating with each other via phone lines, satellite links, wireless networks, and cable systems.

Internet service provider (ISP) A company that provides an Internet connection to individuals or companies.

self-esteem Confidence in one's own worth or abilities; self-respect.

social networking site An online service that brings people together by organizing them around a common interest and provides them with interactive photos, blogs, and messaging systems; examples include Facebook and Myspace.

spam Unsolicited electronic mail sent from someone the recipient does not know.

text message A written message sent by cell phone.

Kids' Internet Safety Alliance
WaterPark Place
20 Bay Street, 12th Floor, Suite 37
Toronto, ON M5J 2N8
Canada
(416) 850-1449
Web site: http://www.kinsa.net
The Kids' Internet Safety Alliance helps to protect children and
teen victims of cyber abuse by educating the public, policy
makers, and law enforcement.

Megan Meier Foundation
17295 Chesterfield Airport Road, Suite 200
Chesterfield, MO 63005
(636) 777-7823
Web site: http://meganmeierfoundation.cwsit.org
The Megan Meier Foundation teaches children, parents, and
educators about the prevention of the bullying and cyberbullying of youth.

National Association of Students Against Violence Everywhere
322 Chapanoke Road, Suite 110
Raleigh, NC 27603
(866) 343-7283
Web site: http://www.nationalsave.org
This public nonprofit organization strives to decrease the potential
for violence by engaging students in violence prevention efforts
within their school and community.

PACER's National Bullying Prevention Center
8161 Normandale Boulevard
Bloomington, MN 55437
(888) 248-0822
Web site: http://www.pacer.org/bullying
PACER's National Bullying Prevention Center unites, engages, and educates communities nationwide to address bullying through creative, relevant, and interactive resources. This organization has named October as the National Bullying Prevention Month.

United States Department of Health and Human Services
200 Independence Avenue SW
Washington, DC 20201
(877) 696-6775
Web site: http://www.stopbullying.gov
StopBullying.gov provides information from various government agencies on how children, teens, parents, educators, and others in the community can prevent or stop bullying.

United States Department of Justice
950 Pennsylvania Avenue NW
Washington, DC 20530-0001
(202) 514-2000
Web site: http://www.justice.gov
The United States Department of Justice provides information about cyberbullying and federal leadership in preventing and controlling crime.

HOTLINES

Anti-Cyberbullying Hotline, Boston Public Health Commission
 (617) 534-5050
Boys Town National Hotline (800) 448-3000
CrisisLink (888) 644-5886
Kids Help Hotline (Canada) (800) 668-6868
KUTO (Kids Under Twenty-One) Crisis Help (888) 644-5886
National Suicide Hotline (800) 784-2433
National Suicide Prevention Lifeline (800) 273-8255
National Youth Crisis Hotline (800) 448-4663
Teen Line (800) 852-8336
Trevor Lifeline for Gay, Lesbian, and Bisexual Youth (866) 488-7386
24-Hour Addiction Helpline (877) 579-0078
Youth America Hotline (877) 968-8454

WEB SITES

Due to the changing nature of Internet links, Rosen Publishing has developed an online list of Web sites related to the subject of this book. This site is updated regularly. Please use this link to access the list:

http://www.rosenlinks.com/beat/cyber

FOR FURTHER READING

Allman, Toney. *Mean Behind the Screen: What You Need to Know About Cyberbullying*. Mankato, MN: Compass Point Books, 2009.

Bott, Christie Jo. *More Bullies in More Books*. Lanham, MD: Scarecrow Press, 2009.

Breguet, Teri. *Frequently Asked Questions About Cyberbullying*. New York, NY: Rosen Publishing Group, Inc., 2007.

Casanova, Mary. *Chrissa Stands Strong*. Middleton, WI: American Girl, 2009.

Cindrich, Sharon Miller. *A Smart Girl's Guide to the Internet: How to Connect with Friends, Find What You Need, and Stay Safe Online*. Middleton, WI: American Girl, 2009.

Conifer, Dave. *eBully*. Charleston, SC: CreateSpace, 2010.

Criswell, Patti Kelley. *Stand Up for Yourself & Your Friends: Dealing with Bullies and Bossiness, and Finding a Better Way*. Middleton, WI: American Girl, 2009.

Fox, Dan. *Bullying and Hazing*. Farmington Hills, MI: Greenhaven Press, 2008.

Friedman, Lauri S., ed. *Bullying: An Opposing Viewpoints Guide*. Farmington Hills, MI: Greenhaven Press, 2011.

Friedman, Lauri S. *Cyberbullying*. Farmington, Hills, MI: Greenhaven Press, 2010.

Green, Susan Eikov. *Don't Pick On Me*. Oakland, CA: New Harbinger Publications, 2010.

Guillain, Charlotte. *Coping with Bullying*. Chicago, IL: Heinemann Library, 2011.

Hunter, Nick. *Cyber Bullying*. Chicago, IL: Heinemann Library, 2012.

Jacobs, Thomas A. *Teen Cyberbullying Investigated: Where Do Your Rights End and Consequences Begin?* Minneapolis, MN: Free Spirit Publishing, 2010.

Jakubiak, David J. *A Smart Kid's Guide to Online Bullying*. New
    York, NY: PowerKids Press, 2010.

Keene, Carolyn. *Secret Identity*. New York, NY: Aladdin, 2009.

MacEachern, Robyn. *Cyberbullying: Deal with It and Ctrl Alt Delete
    It*. Toronto, ON: Lorimer, 2011.

McQuade, Samuel, and Marcus K. Rogers. *Cyberstalking and
    Cyberbullying*. New York, NY: Chelsea House Publishers, 2011.

McQuade, Samuel, and Marcus K. Rogers. *Living with the Internet*.
    New York, NY: Chelsea House Publishers, 2011.

Simmons, Danette. *Teen Reflections: My Life, My Journey, My
    Story*. Charleston, SC: CreateSpace, 2010.

American Academy of Pediatrics. *CyberSafe: Protecting and Empowering Kids in the Digital World of Texting, Gaming, and Social Media*. Elk Grove Village, IL: American Academy of Pediatrics, 2011.

Beane, Allan L. *Protect Your Child from Bullying: Expert Advice to Help You Recognize, Prevent, and Stop Bullying Before Your Child Gets Hurt*. San Francisco, CA: Jossey-Bass, 2008.

Canada Safety Council. "Cyber Bullying." October 19, 2010. Retrieved September 16, 2011 (http://canadasafetycouncil.org/news/cyber-bullying).

Centers for Disease Control and Prevention. "Electronic Aggression: Technology and Youth Violence." August 30, 2011. Retrieved September 12, 2011 (http://www.cdc.gov/ViolencePrevention/youthviolence/electronicaggression).

Hinduja, Sameer, and Justin W. Patchin. "Cyberbullying and Suicide." 2010. Retrieved September 14, 2011 (http://www.cyberbullying.us/cyberbullying_and_suicide_research_fact_sheet.pdf).

Hinduja, Sameer, and Justin W. Patchin. "Cyberbullying: Identification, Prevention, and Response." 2010. Retrieved September 15, 2011 (http://www.cyberbullying.us/Cyberbullying_Identification_Prevention_Response_Fact_Sheet.pdf).

Hinduja, Sameer, and Justin W. Patchin. "State Cyberbullying Laws." September 2011. Retrieved October 1, 2011. (http://www.cyberbullying.us/Cyberbullying_Identification_Prevention_Response_Fact_Sheet.pdf).

Hu, Winnie. "Bullying Law Puts New Jersey Schools on the Spot." *New York Times*, August 30, 2011. Retrieved August 31, 2011 (http://www.nytimes.com/2011/08/31/nyregion/bullying-law-puts-new-jersey-schools-on-spot.html?pagewanted=all).

Kowalski, Robin M., and Susan P. Limber. "Electronic Bullying Among Middle School Students." *Journal of Adolescent Health*, 2007. Retrieved September 2, 2011 (http://www.jahonline.org/webfiles/images/journals/jah/zaq11207000S22.pdf).

Lenhart, Amanada. "Cyberbullying." 2011. Retrieved September 12, 2011 (http://www.pewinternet.org/Reports/2007/Cyberbullying.aspx).

McQuade, Samuel C., James P. Colt, and Nancy B. B. Meyer. *Cyber Bullying: Protecting Kids and Adults from Online Bullies*. Westport, CT: Praeger Publishers, 2009.

Mulvihill, Geoff, and David Crary. "With Teen's Suicide Comes Spotlight, Caution." *Wall Street Journal*, September 22, 2011. Retrieved September 29, 2011 (http://online.wsj.com/article/APfb480cb288524568a66de88e51692a31.html).

National Center for Mental Health Promotion and Youth Violence Prevention. "Preventing Cyberbullying in Schools and the Community." June 20, 2011. Retrieved September 25, 2011 (http://www.promoteprevent.org/publications/prevention-briefs/preventing-cyberbullying-schools-and-community).

National Crime Prevention Association. "Cyberbullying." 2001. Retrieved September 9, 2011 (http://www.ncpc.org/cyberbullying).

OnGuardOnline.gov. "Cyberbullying." September 2011. Retrieved September 25, 2011 (http://onguardonline.gov/articles/0028-cyberbullying).

OnGuardOnline.gov. "Kids and Socializing Online." September 2011. Retrieved September 25, 2011 (http://onguardonline.gov/articles/0012-kids-and-socializing-online).

OnGuardOnline.gov. "Kids and Virtual Worlds." September 2011. Retrieved September 25, 2011 (http://onguardonline.gov/ articles/0030-kids-and-virtual-worlds).

Rogers, Vanessa. *Cyberbullying: Activities to Help Children and Teens to Stay Safe in a Texting, Twittering, Social Networking World*. Philadelphia, PA: Jessica Kingsley Publishers, 2010.

Shariff, Shaheen, and Andrew W. Churchill. *Truths and Myths of Cyber-Bullying*. New York, NY: Peter Lang Publishing, 2009.

Willard, Nancy. "Educator's Guide to Cyberbullying and Cyberthreats." Center for Safe and Responsible Internet Use, April 2007. Retrieved September 15, 2011 (http://csriu.org/ cyberbully/docs/cbcteducator.pdf).

ABOUT THE AUTHOR

Judy Monroe Peterson has earned two master's degrees and is the author of more than sixty educational books for young people. She is a former health care, technical, and academic librarian and college faculty member; a biologist and research scientist; and curriculum editor with more than twenty-five years of experience. She has taught courses at 3M, the University of Minnesota, and Lake Superior College. Currently, she is a writer and editor of K–12 and post–high school curriculum materials on a variety of subjects, including biology, life science, and the environment.

PHOTO CREDITS

Cover © istockphoto.com/Derek Latta; p. 5 © Rawdon Wyatt/Alamy; p. 8 Brendan O'Sullivan/Photolibrary/Getty Images; p. 9 Andrew Bret Walli/Photographer's Choice RF/Getty Images; p. 11 istockphoto.com/Carri Keill; p. 14 istockphoto.com/Kurt Gordon; p. 16 Lisa F. Young/Shutterstock; p. 18 Peter Close/Shutterstock; p. 21 Allison Long/MCT/Newscom; p. 24 © Bob Daemmrich/The Image Works; p. 25 © Rob Nelson/PhotoEdit; p. 30 Emmanuel Dunand/AFP/Getty Images; p. 31 Reprinted with permission, New York: Anti-Defamation League, © 2011, www.adl.org, all rights reserved; p. 34 © AP Images; back cover background, interior graphics © istockphoto.com/aleksandar velasevic.

Designer: Nicole Russo; Editor: Kathy Kuhtz Campbell;
Photo Researcher: Marty Levick